COLLEGE FOOTBALL HOT STREAKS

BY TODD KORTEMEIER

MOMENTUM

Published by The Child's World®
1980 Lookout Drive • Mankato, MN 56003-1705
800-599-READ • www.childsworld.com

Photographs ©: Kevin Reece/AP Images, cover, 1;
Scott Donaldson/Icon Sportswire/AP Images, 5;
David Longstreath/AP Images, 6; Itsuo Inouye/AP
Images, 8; Red Line Editorial, 9; Jonathan Daniel/
Stringer/Getty Images Sport/Getty Images, 10;
Tim Johnson/AP Images, 13; Al Golub/AP Images,
14; Stefan Savoia/AP Images, 16; Jason Mowry/
Icon Sportswire/AP Images, 20, 23; Juan Lainez/
Marinmedia.org/Cal Sports Media/AP Images, 24;
Chris Williams/Icon Sportswire/AP Images, 27;
Adam Davis/Icon Sportswire/AP Images, 28

ISBN 9781503832312
LCCN 2018963096

Printed in the United States of America
PA02422

ABOUT THE AUTHOR

Todd Kortemeier is a writer and journalist from Minneapolis. He is a graduate of
the University of Minnesota's School of Journalism & Mass Communication.

CONTENTS

MOMENTUM

FAST FACTS

How Is College Football Structured?

► College football is divided into three divisions. The highest level is Division I. Within this division is the Football Bowl Subdivision (FBS). It features all the top teams. Those teams play in **bowl games** at the end of the season. Three of those bowl games make up the College Football Playoff, which determines the national champion.

Division I FBS

► FBS features 130 teams. Most are part of a **conference**. Each conference determines a champion. Teams that do not finish with a losing record may be selected to play in a bowl game after the regular season. The top four teams in the country are chosen for the College Football Playoff.

What Is the College Football Playoff?

► The College Football Playoff decides the FBS national champion. It was first played after the 2014 season. A 13-member committee chooses four teams at the end of the regular season for the playoff. They are ranked from 1 to 4.

**The Clemson Tigers beat the Alabama Crimson ►
Tide in the College Football Playoff National
Championship after the 2016 season.**

CHAPTER ONE

SANDERS RUNS FREE

All eyes at the 1988 Holiday Bowl were on Oklahoma State running back Barry Sanders. Sanders burst past the Wyoming defense and with a quick step was off down the field. He left defenders gasping for air. Sanders capped off a record-setting season with 222 rushing yards and five touchdowns in the game.

Sanders's hot streak had begun at the start of the season. Against Miami (Ohio), Sanders returned the opening kickoff 100 yards for a touchdown. He was out of breath from his long sprint down the field, but he felt triumphant. During that game, Sanders went on to run for two more touchdowns. And that was just the start.

The 178 rushing yards Sanders piled up against Miami were his fourth-lowest total of his season. He seemed unstoppable.

◄ **Barry Sanders slips past a Texas A&M defender and races toward the end zone.**

▲ **To opposing defenders, it seemed as though Sanders was untouchable during the 1988 season.**

He rushed for at least 154 yards in every game that year. And he scored at least two touchdowns in each game. In the third game of the season, Sanders really broke out. Against Tulsa, he racked up 304 rushing yards and five touchdowns. That was a school record for yardage.

At Kansas State on October 29, Sanders rushed for 320 yards. On December 3 against Texas Tech, he piled up 332 yards on the ground. Starting with the Kansas State game, Sanders went on a six-game streak of more than 200 yards per game. Opponents could only hope to slow him down.

Sanders set 34 college records in 1988. He rushed for 2,628 yards and had 37 touchdowns. But he technically had more.

At the time, the National Collegiate Athletic Association (NCAA) didn't count bowl game stats for a player's season. But with the Holiday Bowl, Sanders racked up a total of 2,850 yards and 44 touchdowns. As of 2018, no player had come close to hitting either mark.

SANDERS'S 1988 RUSHING TOTALS

DATE	OPPONENT	RUSHING YARDS
September 10	Miami (Ohio)	178
September 24	Texas A&M	157
October 1	Tulsa	304
October 8	Colorado	174
October 15	Nebraska	189
October 22	Missouri	154
October 29	Kansas State	320
November 5	Oklahoma	215
November 12	Kansas	312
November 19	Iowa State	293
December 3	Texas Tech	332
December 30	Wyoming (at Holiday Bowl)	222

CHAPTER TWO

KLINGLER SETS RECORDS

University of Houston Cougars quarterback David Klingler threw the ball with such force that it flew down the green field. Once, when Klingler was a freshman, a teammate needed nine stitches to close a wound caused by one of his passes. "From 25 yards away, I can throw the ball hard enough that you'd be better off trying to get out of the way than you would be trying to catch it," Klingler said.[1]

Fortunately, Houston had plenty of receivers who could catch. The 1990 Cougars possessed an incredible offense. The team had many dominant receivers. Because of the way their offense worked, Klingler could spread the ball around. Six Cougars caught at least 35 passes in 1990. Houston threw the ball so often, Klingler often did not know what his stats were until after a game.

◀ **David Klingler directed the Houston offense in 1990.**

The Cougars led the country in scoring with an average of 46.5 points per game in 1990. Houston raced out to an 8–0 record to open the season. Included in that was one of Klingler's most legendary performances. He completed 48 of 76 passes on a windy October day at Southern Methodist University to keep the Cougars' winning streak alive.

The last Southwest Conference game of the season was the biggest. No. 3 Houston faced the No. 14 Texas Longhorns in Austin, Texas. The Cougars had **routed** the Longhorns in their previous three meetings, scoring an average of almost 60 points per game. But Texas got its revenge.

The Houston offense never got rolling. During the game, Klingler threw four of the 20 **interceptions** he had all season. The Cougars tied their season low for points and lost 45–24.

FOLLOWING A LEGEND

Klingler had some big shoes to step into in 1990. Andre Ware also set records as the Houston quarterback in 1989. He established Houston's reputation as a record-setting offense. Nobody expected much out of the Cougars before that. Ware tied or set 27 records in 1989. He threw for 4,699 yards and 46 touchdowns.

▲ Klingler discusses strategy with his coach.

Their dream of a perfect season was over. And Texas would go on to win the Southwest Conference.

But the season itself was far from over. Houston's final home game was against Eastern Washington. The Cougars beat up on the Eagles by a score of 84–21. Klingler threw a touchdown pass almost every time Houston had the ball. He ended up with 11, which was an NCAA record.

To close the regular season, Klingler was at his best. Against Arizona State, he set a record for passing yards in a game. The teams combined for more than 1,000 passing yards, but Klingler had 716 of them. The Cougars won 62–45.

Klingler set a record with 54 touchdown passes in 1990. Even without the 11 touchdowns against Eastern Washington, Klingler would have still led the country. It was just that kind of season for the hometown quarterback. Some of the records Klingler set have since been broken. But nobody has put together a consistently hot season quite like Klingler and Houston did.

◄ After college, Klingler played in the National Football League. He played for the Cincinnati Bengals from 1992 to 1995.

CHAPTER THREE

A PERFECT SEASON

T he 2000 Miami Hurricanes had their rival on the ropes. They were up 30–20 on the Florida Gators in the Sugar Bowl. With four minutes, 21 seconds left in the game, they had the ball on the Gators' 3-yard line. Running back Najeh Davenport was not going to stop until he crossed the goal line. He took the hand off and barreled ahead for the score. Hurricanes fans in the stands could taste the victory. They chanted, "We're No. 1!"[2] But the Hurricanes were not No. 1. Florida State got picked instead of Miami to play for the FBS national championship. That was even though Miami beat Florida State earlier in the year.

That made the Miami players determined. Next year, they would not let anything get in their way of a championship. They wanted to go undefeated. And indeed, the 2001 Hurricanes' offense was relentless, averaging more than 42 points per game.

◄ **Running back Najeh Davenport picked up some yards during the game against Florida.**

On the other side of the ball, their defense was just as punishing. They held opponents to less than ten points per game.

The Hurricanes dominated at home and on the road. They opened the 2001 season in Pennsylvania against the Penn State Nittany Lions. Fans packed the stands, dressed in their teams' colors. The roaring cheers of the Nittany Lions fans echoed across the stadium. Miami quieted them all quickly, mounting a double-digit lead by the end of the first quarter. Up 30–0 at halftime, Miami went on to a 33–7 win.

That was only the beginning. The team came back home and routed the Rutgers Scarlet Knights 61–0. Three games later, Miami ended Florida State's 54-game home unbeaten streak. The Hurricanes capped off their home schedule on November 24 with a 65–7 revenge win over No. 11 Washington. The Huskies were the only team to beat the Hurricanes in 2000.

Only one game stood between them and the national championship. They had to go against the Virginia Tech Hokies. Miami built a 26–10 lead in the fourth quarter. But the Hokies got back in the game. Down 26–18, they blocked a Hurricanes punt. Miami players heard the thumps of the ball being kicked and then blocked by a Virginia Tech player's hand. The next sound they heard was the deafening roar of the crowd as the Hokies ran the ball all the way back for a touchdown.

Visions of coming up short again started to worry the players. But an interception from the Miami defense sealed the game. Undefeated, Miami was going to play for a national title.

The Hurricanes played the Nebraska Cornhuskers. It was at the Rose Bowl in Pasadena, California. The Cornhuskers were no match for the Hurricanes. Miami opened up a 34–0 lead at halftime and never looked back. The Hurricanes held Nebraska to just 259 yards of offense and won 37–14. Miami was undefeated.

MIAMI'S GOLDEN AGE

Miami's 2001 undefeated season was sandwiched in between two seasons that were almost as great. The 2000 Hurricanes lost the second game of their season and won the next ten. The 2002 Miami team won its first 12 games before falling in the Fiesta Bowl. The Hurricanes were 35–2 in those three seasons, and at one point the team had a 34-game winning streak. That was the sixth-longest winning streak in Division I college football history. Miami also had a 29-game winning streak from 1990 to 1992.

CHAPTER FOUR

THE BUCKEYES COME BACK

Fans of the Ohio State Buckeyes had high expectations during the 2014 season. During the first home game, a record crowd of 107,517 fans packed the stadium. They watched as players from the Buckeyes and Virginia Tech Hokies raced across the green field below. But it was the Hokies who put on a show. Virginia Tech opened up a 21–7 lead that stunned the crowd into silence. Ohio State mounted a comeback, but Tech went on to win 35–21.

It was the first home loss for the Buckeyes in 25 games. It was also the first time they had lost a home opener since 1978. And they still did not know what they had in their new quarterback J. T. Barrett, who completed only nine of 29 pass attempts with three interceptions. Their national championship hopes were in real trouble. But they were not going to give up.

◄ **Corey Smith of the Buckeyes tries to catch the ball while under pressure.**

The Buckeyes went out the next week and destroyed Kent State 66–0. Then over the next three games they scored 50, 52, and 56 points. All were blowout wins. In a 56–17 win over Rutgers, Barrett passed for three touchdowns and ran for two more. With a strong rushing attack led by Ezekiel Elliott, the Buckeyes' offense had hit its stride. Then, the Buckeyes survived close road wins at Penn State, No. 7 Michigan State, and Minnesota. They closed out a perfect conference season at home against **archrival** Michigan. But Barrett was injured in the win.

Cardale Jones, who had never **started** before, had to start in the Big Ten Conference Championship Game. The Buckeyes didn't miss a beat. They rolled over Wisconsin 59–0, and Jones was named Most Valuable Player (MVP) of the game.

The Buckeyes faced the Oregon Ducks in the national championship game. Oregon had Heisman Trophy winner Marcus Mariota as its quarterback. But it was Jones, the Buckeyes' **third-string quarterback**, who got the job done. He threw for 242 yards and a touchdown, and also ran one in. Elliott rushed for 246 yards and won game MVP. The Buckeyes won the national title with a 42–20 victory. Despite a historic loss and injuries to two starting quarterbacks, the Buckeyes never quit, winning 13 games in a row, including the national title game.

**Tight end Jeff Heuerman struggles to keep hold of ►
the football as a Rutgers defender tackles him.**

CHAPTER FIVE

UCLA BLOWS BY TEXAS A&M

The Bruins were beaten up. Quarterback Josh Rosen limped into the locker room. The players took their halftime break wondering what had just happened. Their team, the University of California, Los Angeles (UCLA) Bruins, was losing at home to the Texas A&M Aggies 38–10. It was the 2017 season opener. They were upset, but confident. They had a whole half left to fight for a win.

The second half was a different story. Rosen suddenly could not miss. The Aggies struggled to adjust. They had a lot of trouble covering tight end Caleb Wilson. Wilson was big, strong, and fast. He and Rosen got the comeback started. Wilson was often open in the middle of the field. As soon as he turned to look at his quarterback, Rosen found him with the ball. He had two catches like that, and UCLA scored to make it 44–17 in the third quarter.

◄ **Josh Rosen fires a pass down the field.**

But the Bruins needed a lot more help. It was time for the UCLA defense to step up.

The Aggies wanted to run the ball and keep the clock moving. But the Bruins defense forced them to punt. The Bruins got the ball back and went 85 yards in two minutes and four seconds to score and bring themselves within 20 points. Wilson caught four passes on the **drive**.

But when the Aggies got the ball back, they showed signs of life. They picked up two first downs and moved into UCLA territory. If they scored again, it would be almost impossible for the Bruins to come back. On a second down from the UCLA 42-yard line, Aggies quarterback Kellen Mond went back to pass. UCLA's Jaelan Phillips burst through the line and took him down. Faced with third down, the Aggies ran the ball and then had to punt.

UCLA started the next drive from its own 4-yard line. It didn't matter. Rosen could not be stopped. The Bruins went 96 yards in just over one minute to make the score 44–31. Texas A&M again worked the ball into UCLA territory, but the Aggies' drive stalled, and they had to try to kick a field goal. It missed.

The Bruins then went down the field in one minute and 31 seconds for another touchdown to make the score 44–38.

Caleb Wilson races down the field against Texas A&M. ▶

▲ **UCLA players celebrate a touchdown against the Aggies.**

The defense stuffed the Aggies when the Aggies got the ball, pushing them 3 yards back. Now down just a single score, the Bruins had a little more than two minutes on the clock to get the win.

Rosen moved them down the field quickly with completions of 11, 9, 6, and 16 yards. Two went to Wilson. With 48 seconds left, the drive stalled at the Aggies' 20-yard line. A field goal wouldn't bring them the win. The Bruins had to go for it. Rosen found running back Soso Jamabo for a 10-yard gain and a first down.

But the clock kept ticking. Time was running out. Rosen had to **spike** the ball and stop the clock. The Bruins got to the line quickly. Rosen took the **snap**, reared back to throw the ball to the ground, but then stopped and looked up. It was a fake. Instead of killing the clock, Rosen threw to Jordan Lasley in the end zone for a touchdown. The Bruins won 45–44.

Rosen threw for 491 yards and four touchdowns—all four of which were in the fourth quarter. It was one of the largest comebacks in college football history.

THINK ABOUT IT

► How do you think players are able to start and maintain hot streaks?
► How do you think teammates can help each other accomplish impressive goals in football?
► Do you think playoffs are the best way to determine a champion? Explain your answer.

GLOSSARY

archrival (arch-RYE-vull): An archrival is a team's fiercest opponent, usually dating back many years. The Ohio State Buckeyes beat archrival Michigan.

bowl games (BOHL GAMES): Bowl games are postseason games that college football teams can play in. College football teams want to be good enough to play in bowl games.

conference (KAHN-fur-uhns): A conference is a group of teams. The Buckeyes had a good conference season.

drive (DRIVE): A drive is the series of plays a team runs in trying to score. UCLA started a drive from its 4-yard line.

interceptions (in-tur-SEP-shuns): Interceptions are when the defense catches a pass from the quarterback. Klingler threw some interceptions.

routed (ROWT-ed): Routed means when one team gets beaten badly. The Hurricanes routed Rutgers.

snap (SNAP): A snap occurs when the center hands the ball to the quarterback to start the play. Rosen took the snap and threw the ball.

spike (SPIKE): A spike is when the quarterback intentionally throws the ball on the ground to stop the clock. People thought Rosen was going to spike the ball.

started (STAR-ted): Started means to enter as a participant in a game. Jones had never started on his college football team before.

third-string quarterback (THURD STRING KWOR-tur-bak): A third-string quarterback is the third-choice quarterback on a roster. Jones was the third-string quarterback for the Buckeyes.

SOURCE NOTES

1. Bruce Newman. "The Kid." *Vault.* TI Gothman,
26 Aug. 1991. Web. 11 Jan. 2019.

2. "67th Annual Sugar Bowl Classic." *Allstate Sugar Bowl.*
Allstate Sugar Bowl, n.d., Web. 11 Jan. 2019.

TO LEARN MORE

BOOKS

Doeden, Matt. *The College Football Championship: The Fight for the Top Spot.* Minneapolis, MN: Millbrook Press, 2016.

Sports Illustrated Kids. *The Greatest Football Teams of All Time.* New York, NY: Time Inc. Books, 2018.

Walters, John. *Inside College Football: Preparing for the Pros?* Broomall, PA: Mason Crest, 2017.

WEBSITES

Visit our website for links about college football: **childsworld.com/links**

Note to Parents, Teachers, and Librarians: We routinely verify our Web links to make sure they are safe and active sites. So encourage your readers to check them out!

INDEX